PHANTOMS OF THE RICH AND FAMOUS

Written by Stuart A. Kallen

Published by Abdo & Daughters, 6535 Cecilia Circle, Edina, Minnesota 55439.

Library bound edition distributed by Rockbottom Books, Pentagon Tower, P.O. Box 36036, Minneapolis, Minnesota 55435.

Library of Congress Number: 91-073064   ISBN: 1-56239-037-6
Cover Art by: Tim Blough
Inside Art by: Tim Blough

Edited by: Rosemary Wallner

TABLE OF CONTENTS

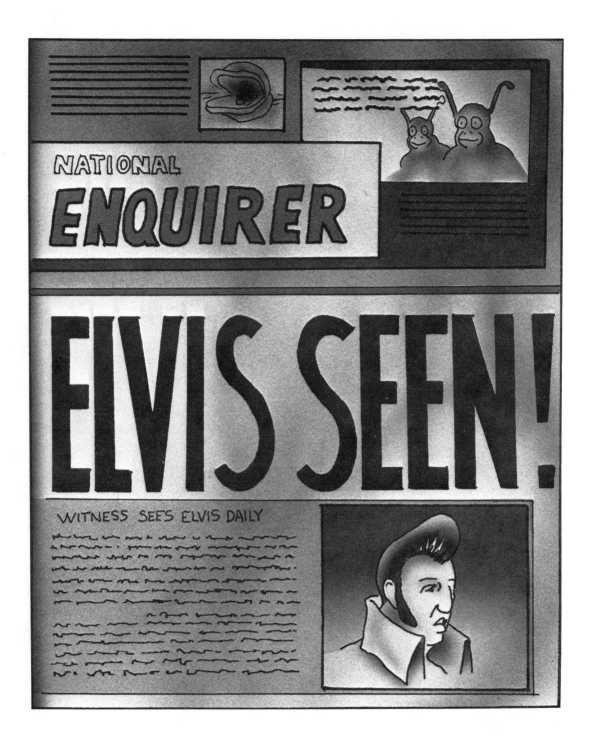

RICH, FAMOUS, AND UNDEAD

They come from the afterlife to visit us — the phantoms of the rich and famous. Voyagers from another world wandering through their old haunts and transmitting cryptic communications from beyond the grave. Some rich and famous ghosts deliver messages of peace and caring. Some famous apparitions want to clear up the mysteries of their deaths. Some spooks just want to ramble through the rooms of their former homes, laughing, cursing, singing, and crying.

Unknown ghosts haunt every corner of the world, but many times their sightings go unrecorded. But when someone sees a famous ghost, the press is notified, psychics are called to the scene, and sometimes books are written about the event. In death, as well as in life, the well-to-do continue to fascinate and astound.

There is a long, long list of hauntings by the rich and famous. Psychic researchers think that when a person dies, their brain patterns and inner thoughts can become trapped in an earthly setting. Then, the bodiless spirit sends mental images to the living. These phantoms may also move objects, make noise, or materialize on the mortal plane.

Many people who are famous are geniuses in one way or another. It is possible that great musicians, writers, artists, and statesmen have stronger mental images that live on after their deaths. From the White House to Hollywood it seems that, in more ways than one, famous people do live forever.

THE MEDIUM GIVES THE MESSAGE

Many ghost stories about famous people come from psychics who are called "mediums" or "channelers." Mediums and channelers claim to receive messages from otherworldy sources. The medium's body becomes the "channel" through which the spirits communicate with us. The spirits might be anyone from extraterrestials to 20,000-year-old gods from India. Some mediums claim they have talked to everyone from Jesus Christ to the late John F. Kennedy. One world famous medium, Elwood Babbit, says he has channeled Mark Twain, Albert Einstein, Martin Luther King Jr., Winston Churchill, Mohandas Gandhi, and Abraham Lincoln.

The White House is said to have many ghosts.

While some people doubt the truth of channeler's claims, many people who have witnessed the phenomenon have no doubts. When spirits take over the mind, voice, and body of the channeler, the other people in the room know something weird is happening. The mediums say and do things that only the spirit would know about. But the medium must be on guard against lying ghosts. An unknown spirit might show up and brag that it is someone famous. Usually a channeler can tell when a spirit is someone famous. Usually a channeler can tell when a spirit is lying by its language and intelligence.

Channeling has become a big business for a few mediums. Rock Kenyon and Bill Kase, two famous mediums, have been written about in magazines like *People* and *Omni*. Kenyon and Kase charge hundreds of dollars to give private readings. They also appear on television in America, Japan, and Europe. "We just sit in the studio," Kenyon says, "and whammo, all these big name spooks come through! Edison, Washington, Galileo . . . the mind reels!"

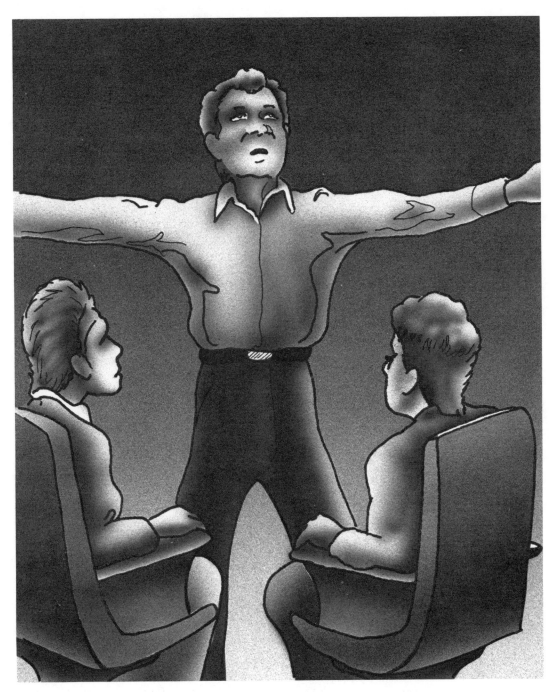

The spirit takes over the body of the channeler.

THE RESTLESS GHOST OF
ABRAHAM LINCOLN

The White House in Washington, D.C., may be the world's most famous haunted house. It's haunted by some of the world's most famous presidents. Thomas Jefferson, the third president, has been heard practicing the violin in the Yellow Oval Room since 1810! The ghost of William Henry Harrison, the ninth president, has been seen wandering about the attic. Harrison died in the White House only one month after he moved in.

The deep, throaty laughter of Andrew Jackson, the seventh president, has been echoing from the elegant Queen's Bedroom for over 150 years. Mary Lincoln heard Jackson stomping around and swearing in 1865, twenty years after his death.

The ghost of Thomas Jefferson, the 3rd president of the U.S., likes to practice his violin in the White House.

The most famous ghost in the White House must be Abraham Lincoln. His ghost has been seen by presidents, staff, and distinguished guests such as Winston Churchill. Queen Wilhelmina of the Netherlands was staying in the White House in 1942 when she heard a mysterious knock on her door. It was the middle of the night, but she answered the door anyway. She saw the ghost of Abraham Lincoln and promptly fainted. The wife of Calvin Coolidge saw the apparition of Abe Lincoln. In 1956, Harry Truman was awakened by Lincoln's knocking. Truman's daughter Margaret also heard Abe's pounding.

President Franklin Delano Roosevelt said he saw Lincoln several times, looking out at the Washington Monument from the Blue Room. One night, the president's maid, Mary Eban, burst into the study screaming. When Mrs. Roosevelt asked what was wrong, Eban said, "He's up there — sitting on the edge of the bed, taking off his boots." Mrs. Roosevelt asked who was up there taking off his boots. "Mister Lincoln!" replied the maid.

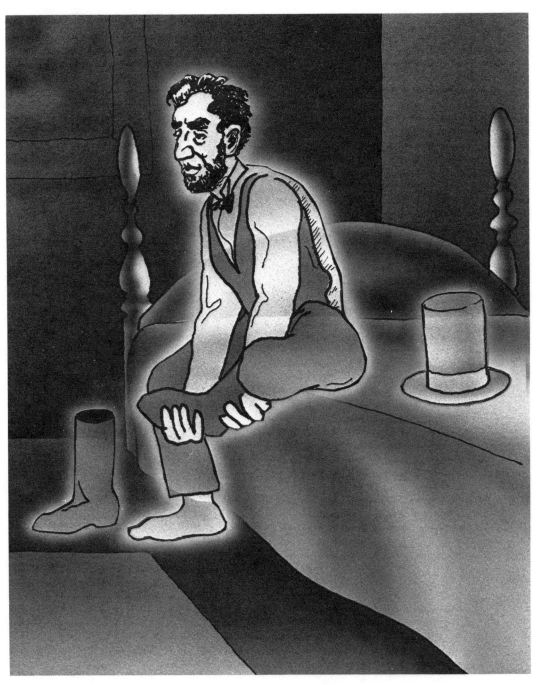

Mrs. Roosevelts maid, Mrs. Eban, was frightened by Abraham Lincolns ghost.

The ghost of the sixteenth president has been seen walking through the East Room, where his body lay in state after his death. He has also been seen staring thoughtfully towards Virginia from the Oval Office.

Both Lincoln and Roosevelt believed in spirits and ghosts and held seances in the White House to talk to the dead. Roosevelt regularly had a medium flown in from the West Coast during the dark years of World War II. People think Roosevelt was asking the spirit world about affairs of state.

At his séances, Lincoln talked many times to his dead son, Willie, who also has been seen in the White House. Some say Lincoln haunts the Ford Theater where he was shot in the head. After Lincoln's assassination (an event Lincoln foresaw in a dream), a train carried his body back to his home state of Illinois. The funeral train, draped with black bunting, slowly rolled from Washington to Illinois. Crowds of weeping people lined up along the tracks to pay their last respects to Lincoln. For years afterward, the ghost of that funeral train was seen. Every April 27 in Albany, New York, people gathered to watch the phantom train creeping down the tracks, carrying the ghost of the president on his long journey home.

The funeral train that carried Abraham Lincoln's body home to Illinois has been seen many times making its ghostly journey.

WINCHESTER'S MAD MANSION

Perhaps the most freakish monument to ghosts is the Winchester House in San Jose, California. The house has staircases that dead end at the ceiling, a switchback stairway with seven turns and forty-four steps that rise only nine feet, and doorways that are only three feet high. The construction was ordered by a woman who believed she was cursed, and the only way to relieve that curse was to build a house to make the ghosts happy.

The story of the Winchester House begins in 1862, when Sarah Pardee married William Wirt Winchester. Winchester's father invented and manufactured Winchester Repeating Rifles. The Winchester's had a daughter in 1866, but she died when she was one month old. Sarah never got over the loss. In 1881, William Winchester died, leaving Sarah alone in her grief and torment.

Sarah turned to mysticism to help her with her anguish. A medium in Boston told Sarah that her husband was cursed. His death was caused by the spirits of the untold thousands of people who had been killed by Winchester rifles. Sarah was about to inherit the Winchester millions along with the curse. She was told that the only way to escape the curse was to buy a house and keep adding rooms to it. The house should be built to please the ghosts, and they would leave Sarah in peace.

In 1884, Sarah bought an eight-room farmhouse in San Jose, California. Within six months, she had expanded the house to twenty-six rooms. The work went on **twenty-four hours a day for thirty-eight years!** The construction stopped the minute Sarah died in 1922. Rows of half-pounded nails can be seen where carpenters stopped working when word came that the eighty-five-year-old woman had died.

The scope of Sarah's hysterical building is mind boggling. At a cost of $5.5 million, the Victorian mansion covered six acres and grew to 160 rooms! There are beautifully carved woodwork, curved turrets and balconies, miles of hallways, eccentric arches, and ornamental everything. The house has 10,000 windows, 950 doors, 47 fireplaces (she thought ghosts liked fireplaces), 17 chimneys (they also liked chimneys), 40 bedrooms, 40 staircases, and 52 skylights.

Sarah was obsessed with the number thirteen. There were thirteen bathrooms with thirteen steps into them, thirteen windows and doors in the thirteenth bedroom, thirteen cupolas in the greenhouse. Those are just a few of the thirteen things — Sarah signed her will thirteen times.

Naturally, the Winchester house is just creeping and crawling with ghosts. There are invisible workmen, photos of ghosts, cold spots, a shaking floor, phantom piano music, turning doorknobs, the odor of haunted chicken soup, slamming doors, flickering lights, and every other kind of spooky phenomenon one could imagine. The ghost of Sarah herself has been seen dozens of times, including at a séance that took place at midnight on Halloween in 1975. Nowadays you're more likely to stumble over tourists than ghosts in the Winchester House. It has been open to the public since 1922.

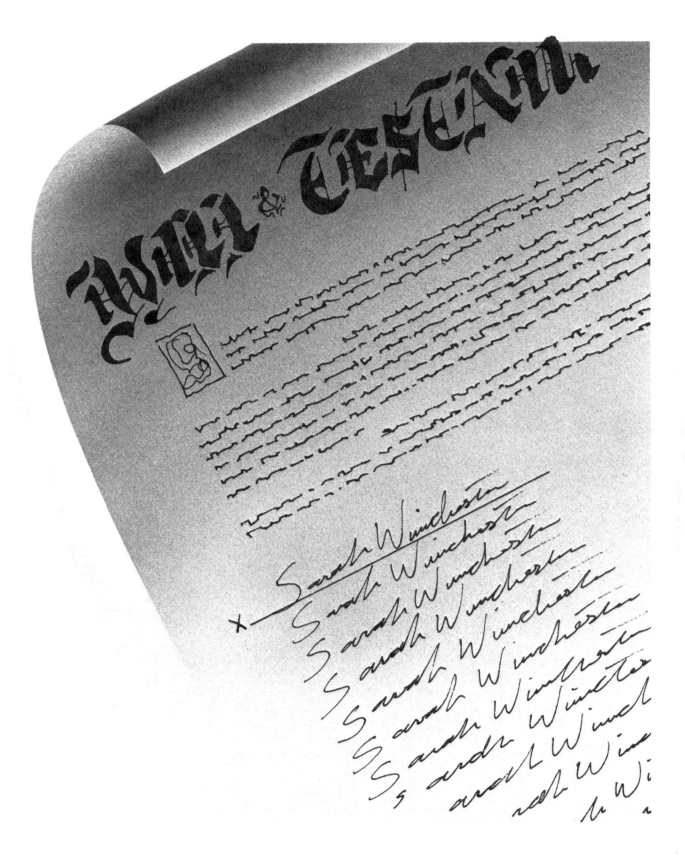

Rosemary Brown plays music composed by ghosts.

THE CASE OF THE
GHOSTLY COMPOSERS

When Rosemary Brown was seven years old, she saw a very old man with white hair and a beard. The old man was composer Franz Liszt and he had been dead for fifty years. Liszt told Rosemary, "When you grow up, I will come back and give you music." Brown was not afraid, she had been seeing what she calls "discarnate beings" since she was a tiny child.

Rosemary Brown grew up in a poor neighborhood in London, got married, had two children, became a widow, and barely made ends meet working in the kitchen of a school. She took piano lessons for several years and knew the keyboard, but could not play very well. One day in 1964, Brown was playing the piano when she lost control of her hands. She looked up and saw Liszt was there, guiding her hands.

Since that day, Rosemary Brown has written hundreds of symphonies in the styles of long-dead composers. Not only had Liszt made good on his promise to return, but he brought along many of his friends. Brown has written symphonies by

Beethoven, Schubert, Bach, Chopin, Brahms, Debussy, Rachmaninoff, and others. She even finished Schubert's "Unfinished Symphony." Brown says Schubert let her hear the music by telepathy.

At the composers' urgings, Brown went public with her talents, demonstrating her powers to London psychic groups. Before long, she became "world famous" when she was interviewed on British television, and the CBS news show "60 Minutes." She was also written about in *Time* and *Newsweek*.

How do composers tell her what to write? Brown says that Chopin tells her the notes and then pushes her hands down on the right keys. Schubert tries to sing the notes but, "he doesn't have a very good voice," she admits. Beethoven and Bach have her sit at a table with paper and pencil while they dictate the notes. The spirits don't just limit themselves to writing music. One day Chopin appeared and excitedly told Brown that her daughter had left the bathtub running upstairs and a flood was about to ensue. Chopin also accompanied Brown to concerts and gave her moral support.

Many famous composers, including Bach and Mozart, play music through Rosemary Brown.

The ghosts also change their appearances. When Liszt first materialized, he was an old man so Brown would recognize him. Then, Liszt became younger and started dressing in modern clothes. Brown says he loves television, and sometimes goes shopping with her. Once, Liszt flipped an apple out of her hand and said she was eating too much! Liszt also brought Albert Einstein to visit Brown. She said that Einstein tried to give her some abstract ideas but she didn't understand them.

Brown has her critics, but many scholars have studied her work and said that it seems authentic. Brown is only a poor to average piano player with little previous knowledge of musical notation. She thinks that the composers chose her because she is psychic and has just enough ability to follow their orders. Because she is such an average piano player, how else could she compose complicated classical music? One respected British composer stated simply, "You can't fake music like this."

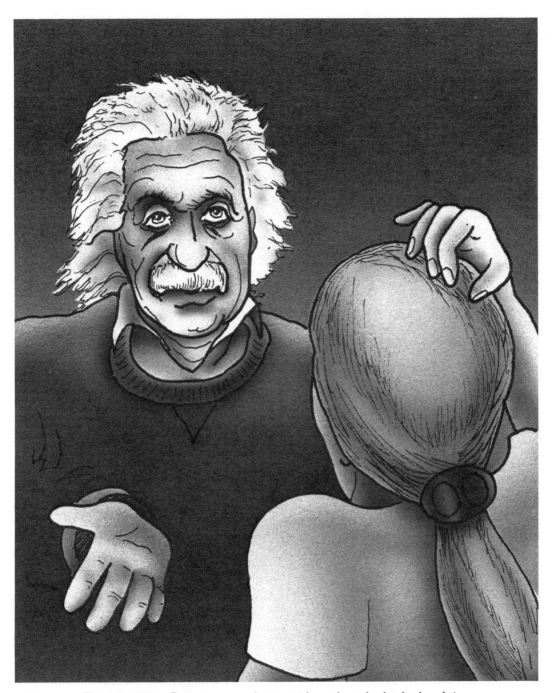

Einstein giving Brown some abstract ideas that she had a hard time understanding.

THE PHANTOM OF ELVIS

To many people, Elvis Presley will always be "The King." His die-hard fans continue to flock to his grave in Memphis, Tennessee; thousands celebrate his birthday every year. For a while, Elvis sightings were an everyday occurrence. Since his death in 1977, Elvis has been spotted everywhere, from Graceland, his home in Memphis, to a fast-food hamburger joint in Michigan. At least one young lady channels Elvis.

Belita Adair is a professional ice skater. In the late-1970s, although she was only fifteen years old, Adair got a job working as a showgirl in an ice show at the International Hilton in Las Vegas. Elvis had played the Hilton many times during his life.

During rehearsal for the show, Adair found herself strangely attracted to a certain dressing room in the Hilton's basement. Adair begged the show's producer to let her into the dressing room for a few minutes. When she entered the room, she immediately sat down at the piano and entered into a very deep trance. According to the producer, Adair became Elvis. She began playing the piano and singing in Elvis' voice. Elvis had recently died, and through Adair, he apologized to his fans for the harm he had done himself, which caused his death.

Before the eyes of her astounded producer and the gathering crowd, Adair's face changed into Elvis'. The music continued as Elvis sang that he was happy where he was. The words rhymed as if they had been well thought-out before hand. After she came out of her trance, her producer asked her, "How could you do that?" Adair replied, "I didn't do it. That was Elvis. I cannot take credit for that."

John Lennon, is said to have sent many messages from the spirit world.

A MESSAGE OF PEACE
FROM JOHN LENNON

On the evening of December 8, 1980, the world famous rock star, John Lennon, was shot to death. The murder took place in front of his home, the Dakota apartment building in New York City. As millions of Beatles fans mourned his passing, John Lennon's ghost began contacting dozens of mediums and channelers all over the world. At the Hong Kong apartment of Beatles photographer Bob Freeman, Lennon's picture fell off the wall, crashing to the floor at the exact instant he was shot. In Los Angeles, a woman who was upset over Lennon's death asked herself what she could do. Suddenly, her record collection scattered to the floor. A Beatles album flew off the stack and hit her in the face. The title of the album was *"Let It Be."*

Since his death, over two hundred people claim to have seen or talked to John Lennon. There have been dozens of books and tapes released of Lennon's conversations with channelers.

Psychic Linda Deer Domnitz says that four days after Lennon's death, he appeared at her Arizona home and began to speak to her. Domnitz wrote a book about her experiences. She also says that some of her friends have seen and talked to Lennon while reading her book. One friend, Robert Shields, was reading Domnitz's book at an airport in India when he saw Lennon. When Shields asked Lennon to prove himself. Lennon knocked him off his chair. The next day, Shields asked for another demonstration and, once again, Lennon pushed him off his chair. Then he heard Lennon's voice, complete with English accent saying, "Oh, give me a break Robert. What do you want me to do, appear on the ceiling?"

A woman in Boston, Massachusetts claims to channel John Lennon. When a reporter asked her very tricky questions about Lennon's life, she answered them correctly in an accent much like Lennon's. The reporter claims that it was the first time he ever interviewed a ghost!

Through mediums, Lennon has stated that he keeps in contact with Yoko, Sean, and Julian, his wife and children. Lennon also claims to have been in contact with his Beatle bandmates, Paul McCartney, George Harrison, and Ringo Starr.

The reason Lennon has been in contact with so many mediums, psychics, and everyday people is best stated in his own words: "People think of me," says Lennon. "I was famous. If someone feels very strongly about me and the way I died, and thinks about me and sends me love, then that works like a magnet with me. It pulls me toward them, and if they're perceptive and they're open, then they'll see me, because I'm there."

Another psychic, Bill Tenuto, claims Lennon keeps returning in order to teach the world the message of peace and love. "When everybody gets the message," said Lennon through Tenuto, "there won't be any bombs, there won't be any wars, there won't be any more people lusting after this and lusting after that, getting greedy to have more than they need.

"The world is designed to bring enlightenment. The whole physical world is just a chain of illusions, a collection of pictures, it's not the ultimate reality at all. So rock on everybody. Live your lives. I wish you love. I wish you peace. I wish for you whatever it is you're asking for, and I bless you all. I get to do that because I'm a spirit, eh?"

GONE BUT NOT FORGOTTEN

So now you see that the dead may speak to the living if they so desire. But some of us are not sensitive to the vibrations of the ghosts of the rich and famous. Most of us have not been chosen to carry on their messages. Luckily for us, we have records, movies, and books where the dead still come alive. Beethoven and Elvis will live forever in music. Abraham Lincoln will live forever in history and the minds of millions. When you hear John Lennon singing "Give Peace a Chance," you know that his spirit and his music will always be with us.